The Phoenix Living Poets

THE WORLD'S ROOM

THE
WORLD'S ROOM

By

NORMAN MacCAIG

CHATTO AND WINDUS

THE HOGARTH PRESS

1974

Published by
Chatto and Windus Ltd
with The Hogarth Press Ltd
42 William IV Street
London WC2N 4DF

★

Clarke, Irwin & Co. Ltd
Toronto

ISBN 0 7011 2066 5

© Norman MacCaig 1974

Printed in Great Britain by
Lewis Reprints Ltd.,
The Brown Knight & Truscott Group
London and Tonbridge

CONTENTS

LESSON

He watches a fishbox, say,
or a languid rope
or a seagull at attention.
— What's the matter with a fishbox? So
he watches a fishbox.
He tries to see just what it is.
He counts the slats it's made of —
sides, top and bottom —
and reads, in neat letters,
Return to Lochinver. He notices
sixpences of scales, gone grubby.
And then he's stuck.
He goes off knowing
he hasn't seen the fishbox at all.

Meantime the fishbox
waits till it's night. Then
like a pterodactyl it planes
through the darkness and flies into
the sleeper's mind. It opens
and crams the sleeper inside it.
And when the hammer hits
the first nail on the head,
he wakes with a scream, he knows
what a fishbox is, he knows
what a rope is, or a seagull standing
at its horrible attention.

MORNING SONG

Morning, and something scratches
at the door of my mind.

Inside the door
you walk windy streets, you wash dishes,
you sit with astonishing books in your hand.
I want to praise your movements that are
so musical, so thrifty, and your stillness
that is so musical, so generous.
Though no birds sing, it's as if
birds were singing in the sweetest
of consort and it's your light
that fingers so gently
the brutal shapes and the delicate shapes
of the world. I want to tell you
how impossible it is
not to tell you how impossible
it is to tell you of the mornings
you make of this morning.

Something scratched
at the door of my mind.
I have let it in.
I make you a present of it.

THE PASS OF THE ROARING

Such comfortless places comfort me.
Not my body but I am fed by these ravens
And I'm nourished by the drib-drab waters
That fingerling through the harsh deer grass.
The tall cliffs unstun my mind.
Thank God for a place where no history passes.

Is this ghoulish? Is it the vampire me
Or grandfathers and greatgrandfathers
Specklessly flowing my veins that bury
A hummingbird tongue in these gulfs of space
And suck from limestone with delicate fangs
A delicate vintage, the blood of grace?

Books vaporise in my lightening mind.
Pennies and pounds become a tribal
Memory. Hours assert their rightness,
Escaping like doves from their cotes of clocks
And lame philosophies founder in bogs
That stink of summer in the armpit rockfolds.

There's always a returning. A cottage glows
By a dim sea and there I'll slump by the fireside —
And another grace will gather, from human
Intercommunications, a grace
Not to be distinguished from the one that broods
In fingerling waters and gulfs of space.

PANTHEON

Are the gods odder
than a belief in them?

You're enough for me.

When I in my solitude
think of you — sometimes
what panic.
I seize your image
and you become
mist, zero, a full-face profile
or the flight of a bird
without the bird.
You commit in me
mindquakes,
my cockle boat bounces above
the swirl
of your delicate trident.
You bring me messages
from ambrosial tables
and when I'm asleep
you let fall a drop
of burning oil
on my defenceless dream.

I, atheist, god-hater,
am tangled in your net
of runes and rigmaroles.
You make me your oddity.
— Girl, I beg you,
blow your nose,
scratch your head,
suffer a not too painful toothache.
Then I'll sit back and contemplate
with eyes blazing with reason
the earthly wisdom
of your immortal statistics.

WORDY LOVE SONG

You've a gloomy hand. It unhands me.
Your mind confuses the meaning of "last":
Spring only means pounce, rose mumbles prose.
You make an aster a disaster.

Mistress of sad prefixes, watch
The world's population of friendly nouns
And how mild adjectives roam there, seeking
Them out, with a flash at each encounter.

I'll give you a verb that's full of love
Because it's "love": but though it's love
It's sharp enough to snip the heads off
Imperfect, disgrace, deflower, unlovely.

Then what a singing of sighs, a consort
Of hands and lips. And we'd compose then
(Putting our heads and hearts together)
The tremblingest, truest, long life sentence.

RETURN TO SCALPAY

The ferry wades across the kyle. I drive
The car ashore
On to a trim tarred road. A car on Scalpay?
Yes, and a road where never was one before.
The ferrymen's Gaelic wonders who I am
(Not knowing I know it) this man back from the dead,
Who takes the blue-black road (no traffic jam)
From by Craig Lexie over to Bay Head.

A man bows in the North wind, shaping up
His lazybeds,
And through the salt air vagrant peat smells waver
From houses where no house should be. The sheds
At the curing station have been newly tarred.
Aunt Julia's house has vanished. The Red Well
Has been bulldozed away. But sharp and hard
The church still stands, barring the road to Hell.

A chugging prawn boat slides round Cuddy Point
Where in a gale
I spread my batwing jacket and jumped farther
Than I've jumped since. There's where I used to sail
Boats looped from rushes. On the jetty there
I caught eels, cut their heads off and watched them slew
Slow through the water. Ah — Cape Finisterre
I called that point, to show how much I knew.

While Hamish sketches, a crofter tells me that
The Scalpay folk,
Though very intelligent, are not Spinozas. . .
We walk the Out End road (no need to invoke
That troublemaker, Memory, she's everywhere)
To Laggandoan, greeted all the way —
My city eyeballs prickle; it's hard to bear
With such affection and such gaiety.

Scalpay revisited? — more than Scalpay. I
Have no defence,
For half my thought and half my blood is Scalpay,
Against that pure, hardheaded innocence
That shows love without shame, weeps without shame,
Whose every thought is hospitality —
Edinburgh, Edinburgh, you're dark years away.

Scuttering snowflakes riddling the hard wind
Are almost spent
When we reach Johann's house. She fills the doorway,
Sixty years of size and astonishment,
Then laughs and cries and laughs, as she always did
And will (Easy glum, easy glow, a friend would say) . . .
Scones, oatcakes, herrings from under a bubbling lid.
Then she comes with us to put us on our way.

Hugging my arm in her stronger one, she says,
Fancy me
Walking this road beside my darling Norman!
And what is there to say? . . . We look back and see
Her monumental against the flying sky
And I am filled with love and praise and shame
Knowing that I have been, and knowing why,
Diminished and enlarged. Are they the same?

MESSAGE TAKEN

On a day of almost no wind,
today,
I saw two leaves falling almost, not quite,
perpendicularly — which
seemed natural.

When I got closer, I saw
the leaves on the tree were
slanted by that wind, were pointing
towards those that had fallen.

When I got closer than that, I saw
the leaves on the tree
were trembling.

And that seemed natural, too.

SPENDTHRIFT

A sigh in the space I reserve for coins
To gleam bashfully of their fair future
Turned me into a cat at a mousehole
(I'm just rich enough to know I'm poor).

I'd miss even one of these bashful shiners.
Was one of them sick? Had a sneaking cutpurse
Keyholed in? What was needed —
A cool prescription? or clinking handcuffs?

No door ever opened so slowly
Or revealed less. There was nothing there.
How search for nothing in nothing? I did it
Then rushed out anywhere, nowhere, somewhere.

And anywhere, nowhere somewhere shone
With glints and gleamings, with round sparkles.
Flowers hung sixpences, trees were fires
Of pennies over the sovereign grass.

That's when I stopped being a miser.
I saw that beginnings have no end
And fell out of love with the ghostly future.
Today is Thursday. I'll go and spend it.

She was walking through a green and yellow landscape.
Her ears bubbled with its streams, her seven skins
Were combed by the rough scrapes of bracken,
Her eyes brimmed with ditches and thorns.

She was trying to forget a thing too joyful to bear
By becoming her body only, that made the joy.
She met green moss as if it were a foreign language.
She tried not to understand the flight of a cuckoo.

But the meaning that was the meaning of the joy
Wouldn't let her be. It went into the foot
She was going to step on. It blew her hair
In a visible wind. A stone wall proclaimed it.

Sharing's not halving but doubling. The warm smell
Of myrtle and heather was a signed message.
And a bird was him and a beach was him.
The landscape and she were his clear mirror.

THE BIG TEASE

When the flood went down
Noah was glad
in his gloomy way
and gave thanks to the Lord.

When the ram
made its pitiful noise
in the thicket
Abraham gave thanks to the Lord also.

They thought big in those days.
— Anyone who carried a joke
so far
must be the Lord.

Even Ishmael
had to admit it.

ONE WAY JOURNEY

Warm clay in the stone wants to come back to me.
That Inchnadamph cliff is full of squeaking fossils.
The sun sinks back to helium. The sea
Boils before ice. Oh, the loud primevals!

There was a time, where I take short holidays,
Before man came shooting his morals
At what created him. I can praise
What never was tortured between true and false.

There was no sad mind to weep for cruelty
Before that mountain was belched into being.
Destruction could only create. What a day
When it made that mind, when it made suffering.

Time scuds full-sail towards a foundering
Not to be stopped by the links of Mozart
And space will be spaceless when Rembrandts cling
No more to its idea, to space free of hazard.

— And yet what starveling mind would surrender
A moment's love for a Time before crystals
Or step on a creeping concept? For there
New planets whirl in a space of fossils.

Spectres of spectra beyond imagining
Ghost an idea on, even in a brain's doldrums.
Sad eyes will weep. — And voices will sing
With what unites triumphs and requiems.

RINGED PLOVER BY A WATER'S EDGE

They sprint eight feet and —
stop. Like that. They
sprintayard (like that) and
stop.
They have no acceleration
and no brakes.
Top speed's their only one.

They're alive — put life
through a burning-glass, they're
its focus — but they share
the world of delicate clockwork.

In spasmodic
Indian file
they parallel the parallel ripples.

When they stop
they, suddenly, are
gravel.

HOGMANAY

Murdo gave the cock meal
damped with whisky. It stood
on tiptoe, crowed twelve times
and fell flat on its beak.

Later, Murdo, after the fifth verse
of *The Isle of Mull,*
fell, glass in hand,
flat on his back — doing in six hours
what the cock had done
in two minutes.

I was there. And now I see
the cock crowing with Murdo's face
and Murdo's wings flapping
as down he went.

It was a long way home.

FAILED OCCASION

With words in my mouth I do my Demosthenes
Walk by the sea where little baby breakers
Two inches tall lisp and prattle:
With nothing in my mind I can't even do that.

A sunset flamingly retires. I feel
I'm a black smudge on a precious manuscript,
Not the exclamation mark I'd like to be.
— What's the use of mere elegant feelings?

Elegant? — sirens with raffish hair-do's.
Their singing's over. They unpick my bones.
I'm squandered. Sand is grit between the words
That ought to flute from me, liquid, birdlike.

It's that damned nothing. Lucky Demosthenes
With a thing to overcome. How overcome nothing? —
Good night to the sirens! I leave them combing
Their blue-rinse locks and go mooching home.

WHERE IS NOW?

I see in windows flowers in transformation
And a telescope peering into what's past
And a new poem that's already a folksong
And a friend who has to be a man that was.

Now's not a bulldozer, though it seems like one.
It goes through my life like a zip in a zipfastener
Till one day I'll strip my life off and reveal
The shape of emptiness, the nothing of forever.

HIS SON TO LAOCOÖN

You make a spectacular figure,
you'll be admired
by centuries of connoisseurs.
You, fool, who always pushed the truth too hard,
see what it has brought you to —
and Troy will fall anyway.

And what of me,
me, who was innocent of the truth,
and who will not live to enjoy
the blandishments of evil
for these hideous coils crushing
the ribs round my heart?

I saw the leaf. It grew from the back garden
Into my brain. It was the second last one
Left on the tree, but the other was dowdy:
It was a fire-straw, a crinkling wonder.

Autumn, interfering autumn, had browned it
And goldened it. It looked like a cymbal's
Soft, shattering sound and refused to stop
Clashing for a frosty winter whim.

Easy to say it dragged into my mind
Whole luminous forests. But no. It only was
A crumpling crackle, a gunpowder angel
That hallelujahed, What things are possible!

PROGRESS

That was the beginning
of an idea — what isn't
the beginning of an idea?

Frog spawn glowed
in the ponds in the thickets
and a melancholy hooter made
mastodon noises over the city.
Everything was as usual.

Then the idea became
a myth — a thing
that ought to be stopped.

And ships sidled uneasily
beside hairy wharfs and in a lighted room
someone cried out with love. Everything
was as usual.

And the myth in the idea grew teeth
and iron wings. It clanked
through the air over
its flat shadow.

And legs arms heads were buried
in the rubble of cities. Great minds
rotted black. And everything
was as usual, everything wept beside
an endless column of refugees.
And good minds said No, good minds
kept saying No. And the word
created a silence round it
and was heard by no-one.

FAR GONE IN INNOCENCE

He sows seedpackets and throws away the seeds.
But what imaginary gardens flourish where
He takes the evening in his gaudy air.

He tells no lie but makes another truth
Of what is true and sees in a summer town
A snowstorm skimming tiny doilies down.

The odd thing is he goes clean through a face
And scans it from the inside. Real or fake,
He tells you what you are and no mistake.

He feels his way through life, like everyone,
But never falls; for nothing can eclipse
The suns he carries in his fingertips.

He has a fault, the fault true innocence
Can't know about, in its onesidedness:
He's full of love and yet is pitiless.

And so he's lonely: as though he always lives
In another month than ours and can make free
With every space but the one from you to me.

REVERSAL

She showed me a polished pebble with a salmon fly
Painted on it. Local arts and crafts
Scrabble on beaches for the addled eggs left
By a mountain, varnish it, make it domestic
And tart it up with a minuscule landscape,
An improbable flower or a salmon fly.

How tunes diminish when they become domestic.
Grace notes fall off, the lamentable, sour
Flat note climbs up that ruinous semitone
And there's the tune's ghost — a flabby ghost,
All its bonestructure gone. It tamely
Toddles the house, slippered, domestic.

Once in a peatbog I found — no ghost —
A blue hare's skeleton. It was its self,
Running dead still. . . Girl with the pebble,
I'll put you out in a wildness that'll tune
Bones and bones to glimmer back in you,
My homely nobody, my skin and ghost.

And seas will break on the pebble, the tune
Be restored to a state of gracenotes — for
Wildness is not wilderness. By the fire
I'll watch your true self moving dead still.
And you and I will, in that artful wildness,
Come into harmony out of tune.

GREENSHANK

His single note — one can't help calling it
piping, one can't help
calling it plaintive — slides droopingly down
no more than a semitone, but is filled
with an octave of loneliness, with the whole sad scale
of desolation.

He won't leave us. He keeps flying
fifty yards and perching
on a rock or a small hummock,
drawing attention to himself.
Then he calls and calls
and flies on again
in a flight
roundshouldered but dashing,
skulking yet bold.

Cuckoo, phoenix, nightingale,
you are no truer emblems
than this bird is.
He is the melancholy that flies
in the weathers of my mind,
He is the loneliness that calls to me there
in a semitone
of desolate octaves.

CATERPILLAR GOING SOMEWHERE

Its green face looks as if
it were about to spit — pft.

It moves along a twig
by doing exercises, bend, stretch —

hard to imagine
a potbellied caterpillar.

It looks so active (hard to imagine it
in the lotus position)

and yet, and yet
it looks so melancholy.

Is it because it knows that
when it reaches a green leaf

its jaws will open sideways
instead of up and down?. . .

It's standing erect now — it turns
from side to side

like a retired sea-captain
scanning horizons.

BETWEEN TWO PLACES

Green flasks of light that's a loch, I can't drink you
But I'll take you home cooped up in a brain cell
And we'll have chats on still evenings
When no-one's about and memories become real.

I'll do most of the talking, but you'll be
A true, True Thomas, elvish communicator
With harps chirping tunes just beyond hearing
For dances in knolls, for banquets under water.

I'll have to translate them, being no elf
Nor, for the matter of that, elf inclined.
How my brain will dizzy to stillness, trying it.
How you'll turn to green the colours in my mind.

The firelight will understand, till it dies
And I trundle to bed. Then I'll hear the sound
Of that harp in a green sleep till I awake —
The most untrue True Thomas in the world.

— And that's true, even though my stodgy senses
Stick to the facts and report them blindly —
That heather, gray stone, a reach of water
And a buzzard mewing on a wall of wind.

STAG IN A NEGLECTED HAYFIELD

He's not in his blazing red yet. His antlers
Are a foot that'll be a spreading yard.
The field was a hayfield: now a heifer
And two cows graze there and no dog barks.

That's the outward scene. The inner —
A mountain forgotten, a remembered man.
The deer will return to the hill: but stiller
Than the stone above them are the scything hands.

He felled one, and dreamed of no question.
Leaves shook and the wood was filled
with froggish exhalations.
He never thought of nests
arcing down, of desperate squirrels.

He felled another, and there was no answer.
He was the axe, he said *Thunk! thunk!*
He never dreamt
of indisputable ladies highstepping
from thickets or moonlighting in carriages
down the dark rides.

The space he made grew forward.
He was his own man, his dreamless self
on a lane of trashed branches.

But ahead of him was a low building and in it
a woman with long nails and a smile
not nice to see. She waited for him
with a bad light in her eyes.

BLACKBIRD IN A SUNSET BUSH

Everything's in the sunset. Windows
flare in it, rooms blush.
Cars scatter everywhere — they make the city
one huge pintable. Life is opulent
as thunder.

Only the blackbird there
contemplates
what the sunset's in:
what makes a flower ponderous
and breathes a mountain away.

The gravity of beauty —
how thoughtfully, how pensively he puts it,
charcoal philosopher
in his blazing study.

AESTHETICS

Words with Greek roots
and American blossoms
have taken over the pretty garden.

That speckled concept
swaying in the hot air
sucks the sap from the branches
it dangles from.

The ground rustles
with centipede nouns.
That soft green adjective devours
its leaf
with lateral jaws.

And the gardeners
hiss together as they walk
with dreadful sprays in their hands.

SHADOW, MY GOOD ONE

1

I went with the shadow. I wouldn't let it go.
It sniffed quick as a mouse at a mousehole —
but I was too quick for it to notice me:
it wound itself up and kept on going.

I followed it past an unusual thing these days —
a horse (a Percheron dappled like a May morning
in one of Hopkins's better poems) and the horse
shied at the shadow which nothing else saw.

I expected screaming brakes and policemen
preserving their woodenness. But nothing
even did a heatwave shimmer. It was as though eggs were
not being broken somewhere, in a heavenly kitchen.

Later, and getting tired of the whole affair,
I asked the little girl I keep in a braincell
if she saw it and what it was a shadow of.
She adjusted herself to my size and answered.

I'd forgotten I remember her answer. —
It was the word *You* but it seemed to have
a different meaning. I'm only pleased
that I remembered not to forget to thank her.

Now it's all over, what puzzles me still is
why did the horse shy on its battering sandals?
I often ask myself this, and the answer
sniffs at its mousehole and clockworks back in.

I suppose (a word I hate like spinach)
that one day I'll adjust myself to my own size
and go down that mousehole and find myself, uninvited,
in a party of shadows enjoying themselves.

Till then I won't tell me about it
as I'm doing now, consoling myself
with handknitted proverbs like *Stones sing only
when no-one's about*, or *Wet hens don't cluck*.

2

Once it was in the water. It could have been
a ballooning whale or the other face
of a cloud or something racing from
one of my eyes to the other bright one.

No sailor me, nor a drowned man either.
On a hook I invented I heaped bait
that smelt of desolate skerries and writhed
the way a brain should when it's thinking.

A pleasant evening, I remember. The skin
of the sea twitched with cormorants and eider ducks
and the sun luminously lowered itself towards
its grand exit, with the minimum of sound.

When the dinghy started sliding shoreward
I knew the bait had been taken, though I felt
no strain on the line I had invented. My fingers
burned a bit, but the blisters were inside them.

When we reached the shore, or the shore reached us,
the shadow didn't stop. It lugged the dinghy
through the gentle froth, the popping bladderwrack
and over the roofs of the quite unnoticing village.

When we came to where a loch fadingly smirked
below us, the shadow planed down on to
then into it. I stretched my knuckles
in what was being left of an ordinary evening,

The boat felt warm. Mountains began
their twilight mazurka. I occasionally remembered
to peer overboard where the shadow lay
as flat as patience. Loch water, loch water!

The line I invented dissolved. I stared
at the shadow cloud dwindling down
to a bed-sheet, a plate, a keyhole through which
I saw my own eye looking upward.

3

Oh such weathers and their discolorations!
I see a hazelnut hobnobbing with itself
among its hairy leaves and can't think why
I smell a glove lifted from wet grass.

If only people wouldn't say "Immediate impact",
so that, paddling my clichés
on these intolerable, speechless brightnesses,
I wouldn't (boastfully) say, *Shadow, I glove you.*

And the shadow I don't imagine, the one
in the hazelnut, then wouldn't brush aside
the loving hairiness, nor would I
be stutteringly bemused with its honeycore shadow.

Core of shadow, look, my limp mind
is sad — but only before intercourse
with your willingness. I rest the image of you
in a discoloration of my mind, perhaps me.

Tunes with my claw, that smell
like a kettle just emptied of boiling water,
I receive you with a shadow of hello,
I give you a feather, I know you'll make a bird of it.

And the bird will nest, without knowing it,
in a hazelnut so busy not giving or receiving
that something won't happen, that there'll be no need
for anything to happen. Happenings will be all over.

ONE WOMAN SHOW

She walks inside her skull
admiring and comforted by
the amazing murals:
landscapes and saints, cool
lovers and hot abstractions —
the outcries of men's sensuality
formalised in a grammar
of relationships.

The only room that bores her
is the portrait gallery.
To her, this friend
is more a still life
than two candles and a guitar.
A line and four blobs
are less abstract
than that family group.

As for the mirror at the door —
when she looks into it
there's nothing there
but the beautiful grammar
of a dead language. —
And what hope is there for her
since she denies the looting,
the flames, the raping
of the blithe barbarians
who killed it?

HOROSCOPE

I know there are words I don't understand
like apogee and azimuth.
I know there are diagrams that pretend to be
diagrams of the past and gossips
of the future.

It's my pretty Now I'm in love with
that won't stand still
to be measured. The past
has gone to a far country; and as for the future
there's no future in it.
But my pretty Now, I love her, I love her,
because she shows herself off to me
and will always be faithful.

TWO INTO ONE

The thin sea breeze met a fat one coming
Down from a corrie. What a confusion
Of ideas and smells — mountain thyme
Growing in sea splashes and mackerel flirting
Round knolls of heather. It took no patience —

Girl who weren't there — to invent true parallels
With you and me — my bladdery seawrack
And your moss campion: my watery slither
And your roe-deer delicate pacing: my yells
Blackbacking on barnacles — and you on a hillock

Golden plovering, sweetly sandpiping.
What a croft we'd be, with our own visitations!
It would swing like a bell, between sounds and shapes —
Its complete round voice would spread away, fading
Over holiday sabbaths of hills and oceans.

STILL GOING

Rock like a cargo boat wallowing through
The jopples of heather — and round its bow,
Look, a stag saunters, momentary seabeast,
Splashed with heather, its antlers foamy.

I won't give up being deceived by landscape's
Likenesses and incorrigible metaphors.
They swish long currents in my mind — fancy
A stagnant mind: a crystal of braincells.

And yet all movements so counterbalance
They spin and doze to such a stillness
That moon and leaf jampack together
And the sun's shone on by a glittering snail.

I have a feverish eye — the right one.
The other's icy. With which do I see
The still rock yawing on heathery tiderips,
The stag splashing towards his sea-nymphs?

BETWEEN TWO NOWHERES

I have a small chaos in my house —
a thing easy to come by. I've not
tamed it, housetrained it.
No: I do my best
to enrage it, to cure it of a persisting small
infection of reason. I say to it
Come on, be chaotic! Make the door of my room open
on the door of my room. — That painting above the fireplace,
why shouldn't its birds fly off or land
on its own water, splashing the hearth tiles?
And me — why should I cross the room, why
shouldn't it cross me?

But all it can do
is push my spectacles under a cushion,
change dates in a letter, put an empty glass
in the chair I'm just sitting down in:
I reach for the book by my side
and it's been hi-jacked to the kitchen.

I say, Come on, you can do better than that!
Until I can get so lost in this room search-parties
have to be sent out for me, until I see what's behind me
more clearly than what's in front of me — until
you crack the sad articulations
in my mind,
how can I make something new, something crammed
with dangerous, beautiful possibilities —
something remarkable even if only for
its excess of normality?

We praise the good God for His creation
of the universe. — When are the hymns to be written
in praise of the unimaginable power of the Word
that first made the chaos that made
creation possible?

IN A WHIRL

The cross-migrations going on in my mind!
I'm dizzied blind
And blinded dizzy by those pantomime
And stroboscopic scene-shiftings. Old Time
Rattles his knees and, grinning fit to kill,
Jigs at all angles in the astounded air.
What can I do but stare
And carol won't you, will you, won't you, Will?

An Immanence is what I want, to be
That Unity
That transcendental One I don't believe in.
How give it birth with no place to conceive in? —
My brain cells all are full: their prisoners lie,
Far too contented, on their bunks and grin
Even though I smuggle in
Files and ropeladders in the proper pie.

There was a time Time kept his printed place
In lower case.
But now he's boss and bully and off his head.
He's displaced place and promoted from the dead
His grandpa Chaos — it's terrifying to see
The douce Laws capering in hippy gear:
A jingbang where it's clear
(Good godless God!) that Immanence is me.

GONE ARE THE DAYS

Impossible to call a lamb a lambkin
or say eftsoons or spell you ladye.
My shining armour bleeds when it's scratched;
I blow the nose that's part of my visor.

When I go pricking o'er the plain
I say *Eightpence please* to the sad conductress.
The towering landscape you live in has printed
on its portcullis *Bed and breakfast*.

I don't regret it. There are wildernesses
enough in Rose Street or the Grassmarket
where dragons' breaths are methylated
and social workers trap the unwary.

So don't expect me, lady with no e,
to look at a lamb and feel lambkin
or give me a down look because I bought
my greaves and cuisses at Marks and Spencers.

Pishtushery's out. But oh, how my heart swells
to see you perched, perjink, on a bar stool.
And though epics are shrunk to epigrams, let me
buy a love potion, a gin, a double.

TWO YEAR OLD

Catherine in a blue pinafore
stands on a chair. Dishwashing's over.
She strokes a bottlebrush of clear water
around the sink and says, Red.

She dips the brush in a milk bottle
and strokes again and says, Yellow.
How carefully, how busily
she paints the sink with clear water.

I know she knows it's just her pleasure
to make two worlds of the one world.
There's nothing wrong with mottled porcelain —
but what's the matter with red and yellow?

She loads the brush, that little maestro,
and speaks with the same and such decision
I stare at the mottled porcelain —
her pinafore isn't half so blue.

A LIFE IN THE DAY OF....

In a second
the world cracked like an egg
and gods cycled out, some with devils
on the pillion or the crossbar.

I knew I was staring at a metaphor.

And things like ants swarmed after them,
all speaking in English.
So eagerly they swarmed, though they flinched
from the oceanic light.

The metaphor was winning.

I called to my friends among them
and they looked up with rosy faces
and waved and shouted and kept on
hurrying. The gods
pedalled furiously past me
and dwindled away. And the things like ants
grew bigger and bigger and passed me and
grew smaller and smaller, leaving me
alone
on a metaphor of planets.

Ah well, I thought, life
is a lesson in metaphors
and death
is an education in itself.
And I pulled nothing over me
and went to sleep
for another time.

UNDERSTANDING

It was an evening, one of those evenings
when flutes play audibly and God's thrombosis
isn't too sore, and human fingers
touch human fingers in immortal braille.

And there was an O in my graph, though discursions
dangled from anywhere — from brambles or the pretty
armpits of lambs; and a stone was more
than just a thing for a vole to go round.

The praise is yours, girl: for you made
everything braille for my blind fingers.
Everything spoke you; for you are the word
to which all other words are a footnote.

It was an evening, one of the many
when your meaning was all the others'
and love and pity were the O in the graph
of the world's loneliness, of wars, and disasters.

LANDSCAPE AND I

Landscape and I get on together well.
Though I'm the talkative one, still he can tell
His symptoms of being to me, the way a shell
Murmurs of oceans.

Loch Rannoch lapses dimpling in the sun.
Its hieroglyphs of light fade one by one
But re-create themselves, their message done,
For ever and ever.

That sprinkling lark jerked upward in the blue
Will daze to nowhere but leave himself in true
Translation — hear his song cascading through
His disappearance.

The hawk knows all about it, shaking there
An empty glove on steep chutes of the air
Till his yellow foot cramps on a squeal, to tear
Smooth fur, smooth feather.

This means, of course, Schiehallion in my mind
Is more than mountain. In it he leaves behind
A meaning, an idea, like a hind
Couched in a corrie.

So then I'll woo the mountain till I know
The meaning of the meaning, no less. Oh,
There's a Schiehallion anywhere you go.
The thing is, climb it.

OLD CROFTER

The gate he built last year
hangs by its elbow from the wall.
The oar he shaped this summer
goes through the water with a swirl, a swivel.

The hammer in his great hand
pecks like fowl in the grain.
His haycocks are lopsided.
His lamp stands on the dresser, unlit.

One day the rope he has tied
will slither down the rock
and the boat drift off idly
dwindling away into the Atlantic.

RESOLUTION AND DEPENDENCE

Rain, that was something. It filled the blank
My mind had become and I hate blankness —
I like to be where there's a possibility of less:
It cheers me up, it makes me feel thankful.

So the rain reminded me I had a mind.
With it I examined it. . .It was a surfeit
Had made it spew everything out. How sweet
Are the ministrations (sometimes) of hindsight.

I'll reduce my diet of you, I thought.
Time to give up this gormandizing.
What saintly ascetic hymns I'll sing
On your daily bread, your cool clear water.

The rain thought differently. It sent
A chilling ambassador down my backbone
And oh, the misery of being alone
And starving in a world of plenty.

But my thoughts got together and drank down you
In fiery tumblerfuls till the midnight
Was lusty with songs no saint would write
However illuminated, redly, or bluely.

WAYFARER

After a Greek sea
of imagination I dip a foot
in the Minch
and freeze to the ankle.
After adding to the cairn
on an Alpine mountain
I climb half way up Cul Mor —
and drop panting
in the heather.

The pretty ladies of the world and the imagination
freeze me to the waist —
I stare at them,
panting,
from a distance.

But in what is
your self and my native land
what an easy traveller I am.
Every day is an anabasis, every day
I shout, The sea, the sea!
and come down
to hospitable villages
where fiestas continuously celebrate
the end of a journey that is
the beginning of new ones.

PREENING SWAN

On the green canal the swan
made a slow-motion
swan-storm of itself:
wings moved through wrong angles,
feathers stared, neck
forgot its bones
and a rotted figleaf of a foot
paddled in the air.

Then — one last shrugging ruffle
and everything fell into place,
into stillness, into a classic
hauteur. — The washerwoman
put on an aristocracy
as false as any other one
and, head high, stared at the ridiculous world
through invisible lorgnettes.

DRIFTING IN A DINGHY

Cloud, light, air, water and its depth —
a treble clef, on which
I am my monotonous single,
black breve
on a shining manuscript.

I think of grammar, I think of you.

— Subject, verb object in one,
your meaning is an everlasting
narrative of illuminations.
Yet I can no more analyse
the syntax of your going or parse
your parts of all speech
than I can explain why music
is a narrative of all illuminations except
yours, even though I can't tell
an organum from
a diminished clavichord.

I hum melodiously
in this abstraction of music,
thinking of grammar, thinking of you,
till a woodwind sighs from the west
and my black breve
goes sharp, goes flat, goes sharp.

DROP-OUT IN EDINBURGH

I steal nothing from you.
I am your incandescent heir.
You bequeath me my incandescence.

City of everywhere, broken necklace in the sun,
you are caves of guilt, you are pinnacles of jubilation.
Your music is a filigree of drumming.
You frown into the advent of heavenly hosts.
Your iron finger shatters sad suns —
they multiply in scatters, they swarm
on fizzing roofs. When the sea
breathes gray over you, you become
one lurking-place, one shifting of nowheres —
in it are warpipes and genteel pianos
and the sawing voices of lawyers. Your buildings
are broken memories, your streets
lost hopes — but you shrug off time, you set your face
against all that is not you.

I am your incandescent heir.
I am your morning side, I am your golden acre.
Your windows glitter me, the sheen
on your pigeons' breasts is me.
I glide through your dark streets like phosphorus.

A.K.'s SUMMER HUT

It clamps itself to a rock, like a limpet,
And creeps up and down in a tide of people,
Hardly ever stranded in a tideless sabbath:
A pilgrimage place where all hymns are jubilant.

The starry revolutions around it,
The deer circling in new foundations
Of old worlds, the immortal noise
Of the river ghosted with salmon — these

Are a bloodstream it's a blood-drop in.
Such sharing. Such giving. See at the window
That silly chaffinch, practically talking Gaelic,
And the eiders domestic as farmyard ducks

And the lady gull yacking for her breakfast.
If I were a bethlehemish star I'd stand fixed
Over that roof, knowing there'd be born there
No wars, no tortures, no savage crucifixions.

But a rare, an extraordinary thing —
An exhilaration of peace, a sounding
Grace with trinities galore — if only
Those three collared doves in the rowan tree.

WOODEN CHAIR WITH ARMS

That chair, foursquare, sturdy as a fortress
Being invested by two year old Christopher
(He clambered up and through and on to)
Is as big in my mind as the hill Cul Mor.

Van Gogh might have painted it, solid
Essence of chair but this chair only,
An interjection into now and here
From where Van Gogh went when he was alone.

The authority of complete aloneness!
I sipped my whisky and watched Christopher
Laughing and jumping and landing unhurt
From a height that dwarfed the hill Cul Mor.

SAYING YES IS NOT ENOUGH

Of course I say Yes,
green bird in what branches?

Of course I agree, dusty branch
so still
in what singing?

The hole in my head
is willing, is shaped for
what can be poured into a full jug,
what lurks under the ice of zero.

Green bird, invent those branches,
my mind is hungry for them.
Dusty branch, I have echoes lined up
for that singing.

When a dog runs away
I love that fuzzy film —
the innumerable shapes of dog
he trails behind him.
But the hole in my head
forms itself for
the dog he's running into.

Fulfilment is a sad word
since it helplessly means
its opposite —
I know all about this
since I keep learning
what's left when you empty emptiness.

THE NATURE OF GIFTS

He went as though water were no matter —
He drowned five times a day. He entered fire
As though it were no more than a hostile wish
And walked out in a mist of his own ashes.

The girl with the white geranium wept for him.
A boy offered him an apple all through the summer.
How he turned aside the streams' supplications
And left birds lonely with their lost arguments.

He was king of them all, the fool, of the loneliest kingdom.
Yet out of the time he haunted, out of the dream
He made of things, come at last glimmering only
The white geranium and the so shining apple.

THE UNLIKELY AS USUAL

Green in the grass is a blade of grass
But you in my mind are a fiery cluster.
Milky the stars in the Milky Way —
In my dusty thoughts you're glinting gold dust.

Once I glimpsed in my thickety wood
A crimson unicorn. It snorted bluebells
And piaffered violets and like an angel
Vanished, leaving the air true.

On lucky days I visit that truth
And find you walking there, being gentle
With shades and toadstools and toadstool moss.
Each of these times is a lucky again.

A waterdrop is green in its wave
But you in any of the world's spaces
Deny likeness — and yet you make
The law of likeness a state of grace.

Unicorn, what were you in the shades
With your melting eyes and lifted forefoot?
You reached from myth and gave me a girl
Whose like was never in that wood before.

PRIVATE

Those who recognise my mask and recognise
my words — all to be found in the dictionary —
shall I scare them, bore them
with a truth? Shall I distort
the words to be found in the dictionary
in order to say what they mean
when they mean me?

How my friends would turn away
from the ugly sounds coming from my mouth.
How they would grieve for
that comfortable MacCaig whose
small predictions were predictable.
How they would wish back
the clean white bandages
that hid these ugly wounds.

PROSPECTOR

I go fossicking among
your laughing streams, panning
grits of gold. Insistent as a cuckoo
my knapping hammer clinks
in your peaceful valleys.
I walk among treasures.

I think
If only I could burrow down
layer by layer, fossil by fossil —

but then, then
I wonder
what horrible violence spewed up
that lava slope
in whose quiet valleys
I swish and swirl such gold
from these clear streams.

CONVERSATION PIECE

At a turn of the green road
two rockinghorses met and
passed the time of day and
nodded sagely. One remarked
on the weather and the other
nodded sagely. They discussed
the political situation and the appointment
of an Over Minister for the Under Minister
of Education and nodded sagely.
They remarked on how well each other
looked and condemned the rising prices
of calliopes and roundabouts and
nodded sagely. And at last
with a nod of the most profound,
the most unmeasurable sagacity,
they titupped off, varnishing the green road
with their outward light and leaving
the birds and the bees
doubled over with laughter at the sagacity
of rockinghorses.

BIRTHDAYS

In the earliest light of a long day
three stags stepped out from the birch wood
at Achmelvich bridge
to graze on the sweet grass
by the burn.
A gentle apparition.

Stone by stone a dam was built,
a small dam, small stone by stone.
And the water backed up, flooding
that small field.

I'll never see it again.
It's drowned forever.
But still
in the latest light of a lucky day I see
horned heads come from the thickets
and three gentle beasts innocently pacing
by that implacable water.